SEATTLE DOG

—— city guide for dog lovers ——

SEATTLE DOG

—— city guide for dog lovers ——

The Best Outings for
Seattle & Eastside Dogs

BLUE MOTH
M E D I A

The Seattle Dog City Guide
City Guide for Dog Lovers

ISBN: 978-0-9776470-3-4

Bluemothmedia.com
Bluemothmedia@yahoo.com

Wholesale/Retail:
If you are interested in wholesale discounts for your retail store or shelter, contact Blue Moth Media at bluemothmedia@yahoo.com.

Special Note:
In celebration of the dog-human bond, this book offers Seattle and Bellevue area dogs a guide to places to go, things to do, and the best that Seattle/Eastside offers to dogs and their human companions. It is not exhaustive. Most of what is listed ranked highly in customer rating websites. However it is impossible to list everything and so apologies to the establishments that are left out of this book. Not every restaurant is listed, or dog park, or vet, or doggie day spa because life changes with the economy. Businesses and apps come and go and we cannot keep up. This book provides links to much more information than we could include in this book. We hope that you access the websites included and find the best places to go – for you and for your dog.

TABLE OF CONTENTS

GO!

DOG'S DAY OUT

Tired of being cooped up all day? I'm talking to the dog…

Want to go out? He jumps up and his tail beats the furniture as he runs to get the leash. Ok then. Play time or poop time, its time to get out of the house and romp in the land of the other dogs.

Dogs need a day out as often as you do. Whether to a dog park, a hike in the woods or on the beach, the local coffee shop or brewery, more places are welcoming urban dogs.

In fact, wherever I go, I see more adults with dogs than I see children.

According to figures from the U.S. Census and the Seattle Animal Shelter, there are now more dogs in Seattle than children – about 50,000 more dogs than kids. Dogs ride the local buses, jog with their human companions through city parks, lay at their feet in outdoor seating areas of restaurants, hop a plane in the carryon luggage if small enough, and find doggie spas and dog parks established just for them.

The dog-human bond has evolved into something more than a work animal. They have become the object of affection that transcends human love. Just stroking the fur releases oxytocin, a hormone that promotes bonding and feelings of love, in both humans and dogs. The dog's seemingly unconditional love has rescued many a depressed person and steadied many with post-traumatic stress disorder. The incredible training of medical dogs that detect when their human companion needs medication is amazing. The empathy shown by some breeds actually soothes the emotional ups and downs of life. Dogs are truly the best friend one could ask for – a listener who doesn't talk back, a greeter who wags hello and doesn't care what you look like or smell like – in fact, your scent makes you even more interesting.

In celebration of the dog-human bond, this book offers Seattle and Bellevue area dogs a guide to places to go, things to do, and the best that Seattle/Eastside offers to dogs and their human companions. It is not exhaustive. Most of what is listed ranked highly in Yelp. However it is impossible to list everything and so apologies to the establishments that are left out of this book. Not every restaurant is listed, or dog park, or vet, or doggie day spa because life changes with the economy. Businesses come and go and we cannot keep up. This book provides links to much more information than we could include in this book. We hope that you access the websites included and find the best places to go – for you and for your dog.

READY?

Urban Dog Etiquette

Top 8 Apps for Dog Owners

Traveling with a Service Dog

"Most owners are at length able to teach themselves to obey their dog."

Robert Morley

URBAN DOG ETIQUETTE

The neighbor's dog pooped in my yard again. Its still lying there waiting for me to step in it. I'm tired of asking the old man to pick up after his dog. Another neighbor's cat thinks my raised veggie bed is her personal litter box. I chase her out all the time. Untrained or neurotic dogs left locked up indoors all day while their human companion is at work, tend to bark incessantly, annoying the neighbors. One neighborhood association gave a man the ultimatum – either get rid of your nuisance barking dog or have him debarked. I won't tell you what he did but a good doggy shrink and trainer could have been a wiser investment.

Urban dog etiquette is a must if you plan to take your dog out in public. It is taught from puppyhood onward into adulthood – yours and the dog's. A well-behaved dog and a dog-conscious owner are more than welcome in many public places. An ill-behaved dog can ruin many a person's day.

Here are some tips to help you enjoy your days out with your dog.

DOG GONE LAWS

Leash

Most counties have leash laws to protect both dog and others. When leashed, a dog is safe from traffic and unable to follow his instincts to chase children, investigate garbage cans or dig up landscaping. Whether a dog is friendly or aggressive, a leash keeps him in check and allows the public to pass undisturbed. Some communities have leash-length restrictions. Whether it's the law or not, keep leashes to six feet or less on public sidewalks.

Retractable leashes should not be used in areas frequented by joggers, skaters or cyclists; the thin line blends into the background and, all too often, athlete and dog collide.

License

Licensing a dog enables an animal control agency to return a lost pet to his rightful owner. Also, licensing fees often support local animal control efforts. In addition, the number of licenses issued gives government officials an idea of how many dogs are in the community, statistics that are very helpful when planning dog runs, shelter expansions and the like.

Dog Doo

Pooper-scooper laws are essential for both the health and beautification of the community. Canine diseases and parasites are often shed in feces, which puts other dogs and children at risk. And no one enjoys maneuvering through unsightly piles of dog waste when out for a stroll.

Pick up feces using a plastic bag, and knot the top to control odor and flies before disposing of it in a waste receptacle. Train your dog to urinate in gutters or on nonliving vertical surfaces, such as lampposts or hydrants. Avoid trees and flowerbeds.

Etiquette Lessons

You attended at least elementary school and learned to read or you wouldn't be reading this book. Your dog also needs to learn to "read" your commands – either verbal commands or hand signals. If you are at a loss on how to teach your dog basic etiquette, skip to the chapter on dog training and invest in a good class. It will make your outings more pleasant for everyone.

The well-trained city dog needs to respond to a minimum of four basic commands: "Sit-Stay," "Heel," "Leave it" and "Come." When you're waiting at a traffic light, a dog in a "sit-stay" is out of harm's way. And while walking nicely on a loose leash is enough for most forays, there are times when your dog will need to be at heel position, which keeps her under control at your side.

The command "Leave it" is employed when it is necessary for Fido to avert his gaze. Whether he's focused on an uneaten cheeseburger left on a park bench or a jogger, getting your dog to break eye contact with "forbidden fruit" before he acts enables you to draw his attention to safer rewards and pursuits.

Or, should the dog slip his collar or break his leash, a recall command ("Come") could save his life. Most, if not all, of these commands are taught in basic obedience/manners class.

Remember that dogs can be frightened by sudden loud noises, such as running children, motorcycles, skateboarders and in-line skaters, to name a few. Be aware that such situations may demand quick and complete control on your part to prevent your dog from lunging or biting.

Before leaving home to run errands with your dog by your side, take a moment to consider which places permit dogs and which do not. For your pet's safety, leave him at home when he is not allowed to go into an establishment with you. A dog left tied to a post or parking meter is an easy target for teasing or theft.

If in Doubt – Check Yourself Out

When you ride in an elevator, do you jump all over people? Your dog shouldn't either. When a door opens, do you dash out heedlessly into traffic, or run blindly into others when dashing around a corner? Do you run up and smother an unknown child's face with kisses? If you do, I have another referral for you...

Some people are afraid of dogs. And some people may be afraid of you. Keep your dog close while riding in elevators, walking on city streets, and especially around children in parks. Not everyone loves dogs, so it's up to the urban dog lover to present a dog who is well-socialized and under control.

A little training and thoughtfulness, endears people to you and your dog. A well-behaved dog is welcome in many places and the more dogs that exhibit first class etiquette, the more establishments will open their doors to dogs.

"I hope to be the kind of person
my dog thinks I am."

———

Unknown Author

TOP APPS
FOR DOG OWNERS

Tagg

Where did Fido go? Lost dog's are like lost children. If you love them, you want them back. Tagg is a GPS attachment for your dog's collar. The related app will track your dog's activity and send you a message if he goes beyond the boundaries you set. The GPS setting will give you an exact location on your dog. . Not only that, Tagg allows you to make sure your dog is getting enough exercise by measuring movement.

http://www.pettracker.com
App is free for iPhone and Android.

DoggyDatez

DoggyDatez is a mobile social platform for dog owners and their dogs to make friends. The main idea is that you can "mark your territory" and see who else visits your spot. You're also able to search for other

DoggyDatez users by gender, age, dog gender, dog age and/or dog breed.

Available on iOS and Android.

Pet Phone

The Pet Phone app lets you track your dog's health with ease. You can keep track of vet appointments, medications, allergies and food preferences for each of your pets, and the app can be synced with your calendar to get reminders.

Available on iOS.

iCam

If you want to see what your dog is up to in real-time, iCam is the app to get. You can watch your canine friend remotely, just to make sure everything's all right. This is especially useful if you're leaving your dog home for the first time, you recently moved or you're traveling.

Available on iOS and Android.

Petoxins

It's tough, if not impossible, to know everything that is harmful to your dog. The Petoxins app from the ASPCA helps you out by having a impressive list of poisonous plants, and most of them you probably didn't know. For example, did you know that tulip bulbs are hazardous? Now you can keep similar vegetation out of your dog's reach.

Available on iOS.

MapMyDogWalk

With MapMyDogwalk, you and your dog can get fit at the same time. You can log your walks, track your calories and map your favorite routes using GPS. The app also has sharing and geotagging features for photos and data.

Available on iOS and Android.

Pet First Aid

Raising pets is fun, but it's also a big responsibility, which means there can be some scares. If anything should happen to your dog, Pet First Aid helps you take the right steps to make sure he'll be OK. Detailed videos and illustrations include restraint, muzzling, CPR, bandaging and more.

Available on iOS and Android.

My Pet Minder

Pet Minder helps you keep track of your dog's actions, and it's presented in an easy way so you can use it while interacting with your dog. By tapping custom buttons, you'll never forget when you last gave your dog medicine, fed him, took him for a walk or took him to a play date. You can also track training phases for puppies, set up reminders and share information via notifications.

Available on iOS.

Dog Snap

Dogsnap is the second in a series of electronic field guides developed by scientists from Columbia University and the University of Maryland. This free mobile app uses visual recognition software to help identify a dog's breed from a photograph of its face.

Available on iOS.

Weather Puppy

It's useful to check the weather before you take your dog out for a walk, but Weather Puppy takes it to a new (and very cute) level. The app shows more than 100 dogs depending on the time and weather, and you can even add a pic of your own dog. Weather Puppy partners with non-profits and shelters across the U.S.

Puppy Coach 101

Puppy Coach 101 takes the headache out of training your new pup by breaking it down into nine easy-to-follow topics, like crate training and teaching sits, each with its own set of bite-sized, trainer-led instructional videos. You can keep track of your progress as you go by checking off successful topics—just don't forget to print out your personalized diploma once your pooch passes the entire course!

($2.99 on iPhone)

Dog Park Finder Plus

Dog Park Finder Plus is like the Yelp for dog owners searching for the perfect nearby puppy play place. View more than 6,000 dog-friendly parks, beaches, and interstate rest stops across the U.S. in map or list form, the latter of which shows vital stats like hours of operation, how much it costs to enter, and if it's fenced-in or not. User-submitted photos and reviews make sure you get the inside scoop before you let your pooch set his paws inside the park.

($1.99 for iPhone)

BringFido

Travel easy with BringFido, an app that lets you search for pet-friendly hotels and lets you book your accommodations right then and there. Besides letting you filter your search by distance, popularity, rating, and price, the app also lays out each hotel's pet policy so there are no last minute surprises at check-in (though if any problems pop up, BringFido's customer service agents are just an email away). Once you've sorted your stay, search for dog-friendly restaurants, parks, and even dog-related events happening nearby.

(Free for iPhone)

Dog Whistler – Your Free Dog Whistle

This free app makes training your dog that much easier, with a built-in dog whistle and multiple options. You can change the frequency of the dog whistle and also modify the sound patterns. Possibly the niftiest feature: you can set an alarm that's motion activated and triggers a dog whistle! So once you figure out which frequency is most effective for training, you could, for example, click the motion-activated alarm and set it to trigger a dog whistle when your dog jumps on the couch. Automated training and a better-behaved dog!

Dog Translator

We've all wondered what our dog is thinking – the Dog Translator gives you an entertaining way to find out. The free novelty app for iOS lets you record your dog's barks and other noises, and then gives you a translation (like the example shown above). Good for a laugh!

Pavlov Dog Monitor

This training app ($1.99) is just for the iPad, letting you keep tabs on your dog's behavior while you're gone. It helps train your dog to be more independent and behave better while you're out of the house – great for getting barking dogs to be quieter during the day.

http://pavlovdogmonitor.com

Dognition

Dognition is another app that's web-based, not mobile based. However, the concept is truly intriguing – you sign up, get a set of tests, perform the tests on your dog, and record the results. You'll receive a profile of the way your dog thinks, which you can then use to understand your dog better and train them more effectively. You can choose to pay a monthly fee in order to receive monthly games and analysis, as well as tailored training tips and activities based on your dog's profile.

https://www.dognition.com

"Dogs have a way of finding the people who need them, filling an emptiness we don't even know we have."

———

Thom Jones

TRAVELING WITH A SERVICE DOG

I travel a lot. And everywhere I go I see service dogs. A halter, a vest, or special dog tags usually identify them, however, some are undercover. They walk serenely beside their owner on a short leash and are very well behaved and alert.

On a cruise ship I spied two golden retrievers before I looked up to see their owners. Obviously seeing-eye dogs, I couldn't resist asking the couple the number one question everyone asks – Where does your dog poop on a cruise ship? They laughed and patiently explained the details of traveling with their dogs.

They packed up puppy pads and a collapsible box that they trained their dogs to use as a litter-box while away from home. About a week before leaving on a cruise, they re-trained their dogs. They kept the box on their stateroom balcony. Although the cruise ship supplied a similar set up, they found that theirs was preferable and they were still responsible for bagging it up and getting rid of the evidence.

I noticed another service dog while boarding an airplane. The owner seemed like an ordinary guy with a black Labrador. No special markings on either of them. Airline officials requested no special papers as they simply let them pass through security. After noticing the dog sitting at his owner's feet just across the aisle from me on the plane, I struck up a conversation with the owner. He told me the dog was a service dog for PTSD. He was a veteran of the Iraqi war. The dog had a calming influence on him.

Another service dog on the plane was medically attuned to detect low blood sugar in a woman who has diabetes. The dog was allowed on the plane with little fanfare as well. Apparently, both service dog owners had the system wired to be hassle free when boarding airplanes and it made travel go more smoothly for everyone.

While it is illegal for TSA and airlines to ask what the medical condition is that necessitates a person traveling with their service animal, adhering to certain protocols makes for smoother travel. Both unmarked dogs had papers in their owners' possession that identified them as service animals by their veterinarian, a paper that noted the disability rules for allowing access and federal laws related to traveling with service dogs, and a current vaccination report. It seemed to suffice. If the owner gets hassled, all s/he has to do is whip out the paper that notes the laws and regulations regarding service-related animals.

Generally, federal laws protect people with disabilities to be accompanied by their service animals. No deposits or extra fees may be charged for the service animal. ID or "certification" of the service dog's training, or of the person's disability, cannot be required for access on buses, trains, planes, taxis, rental cars, US-registered cruise ships or to places open to the public. However, it is a good idea to have at least a current vaccine record and some identification for the dog in case of an emergency. And in case your dog has a medical emergency, have a back-up plan for getting you both home.

Prepare your Dog for Odd Distractions

Travel is stressful for humans and for dogs. Some service dogs adapt well to new environments, schedules, food and water; others become distracted or stressed. This can affect their ability to work, their needs to eliminate, their appetites, and their dispositions. The more you can introduce your dog to the conditions he will experience during the trip, the better you will be able to anticipate his reactions and plan for his comfort.

You are responsible for the care and appropriate behavior of your service dog. The better prepared your dog is, the easier the trip will be for both of you. Teach your dog:

How to tolerate being handled by a stranger. If you will be going through security or importation checkpoints, your dog might have to be examined or checked with a metal-detector wand.

How to travel on the types of transportation you will use. If possible, get your dog accustomed to these prior to departure. Include elevators, escalators, lifts, as well as vehicles.

How to eliminate in a variety of situations. The dog that can toilet only on grass might have a difficult time if the only available site is concrete, or if you are stuck indoors and cannot get the dog outside. Teaching your dog to eliminate on command, and to perform in a variety of situations will help you overcome any obstacles to meeting your dog's toileting needs. Teaching your dog to eliminate on newspapers and into a super-absorbent diaper will give you options to use no matter where you are. Place a plastic bag under the newspapers to protect the surface below and make cleanup easier.

Dog Papers, Proof of Ownership and Vaccines

Different countries have different entry and exit rules for service dogs. Proper documentation can take the hassle out of traveling. Top documents include:

- A current record of the dog's vaccination history, in case of incident.

- Carry 2 recent photographs that show your dog's face and body, one close-up and another with the dog standing next to a common object (like a chair) for scale.

- Carry a written detailed description of your dog: age, weight, height at shoulders, identifying markings, license number, and contact information for the licensing agency.

- Carry a muzzle just in case its required and make sure your dog is trained to wear it.

- Make 3 copies of all necessary documentation. Keep one with you at all times. Keep one copy where you stay. Keep one copy with someone at home who can be contacted at any time to fax it to you should you need another copy while traveling.

Keep a tag on your dog's collar that gives some identifying information, such as, "Service Dog" and your last name and a phone number. Make sure this is a phone you have access to or is one where someone will notify you immediately in the event that your dog is separated from you and found.

If you choose to have an electronic chip planted in your dog, make sure it can be read by any type of scanner and that scanners are routinely used where you are going. If your dog is tattooed, carry that number and the contact information for the registration agency.

Get Input from Your Veterinarian

- Find out if there are any diseases or parasites that your dog might be exposed to while traveling, and discuss with your veterinarian what you can do to protect your dog.

- Time zone changes can be as hard on dogs as they are on some people. Discuss whether to alter your dog's feeding and elimination times to adjust his schedule to fit the time zones you will visit. Keep in mind the activity schedule you will have so your dog can be on a schedule that is comfortable for him.

- Get advice about any different nutritional needs your dog might have while traveling, especially if there will be a change in the amount or pattern of work the dog will be doing.

- Ask how long to withhold food and water before and during traveling, to reduce the dog's need to eliminate.

- Discuss whether you need to change the schedule or dosage of any medications your dog needs. Obtain an adequate amount of the medication, and a prescription for the medication in case your supply is damaged or lost.

- Find out if you can depend on the safety of the water supply during your trip, or if you should give your dog bottled water.

- Discuss how to recognize and treat motion sickness (and altitude sickness if you will be in high altitudes) in your dog.

- Get a referral for veterinary services at your destination.

Your Dog – Your Responsibility

Once you arrive at your cruise ship, hotel or other lodging, identify the areas available for your dog to exercise and play. Make sure they are safe for him (no glass, spoiled food, etc.). Do not expect hotel, transportation or employees of other public entities to walk or exercise your dog. US federal law is clear that the service dog's care and behavior is the responsibility of the person with the disability. Many places have policies that do not permit employees to handle service animals because of liability issues. If you will need help, find out if there is a volunteer service or dog care service that you can access where you will be visiting.

Allow plenty of time for a walk and exercise prior to travel.

Provide adequate rest periods for your dog to be off duty.

Traveling with a dog can be like traveling with a child – you can pack light or take everything but the kitchen sink. Choose the items that will help make your trip relaxed and enjoyable!

Dog bowls. In a pinch, one will do for both food and water. Check out the different kinds (metal, plastic, lidded, collapsible fabric, etc.) for the one that will travel best. Disposables will eliminate the need to wash dishes. Purchase dog food where you visit to save luggage space. If you bring your own dry food, packaging it in single portions in plastic bags will make serving easier. The bags can be used for "scooping" later. If you use canned food, remember the can opener.

Don't forget to pack one or two toys that your dog likes. Make sure at least one is not a "noise-maker" so your dog can enjoy himself without annoying others.

A supply of favorite treats can go along ways to keeping your dog calm and happy in odd places. In fact, pack yourself a few of your favorite treats, sit back and enjoy the trip.

SET

Paws on the Bus, Monorail & City Center

Dog Park Do's & Don'ts

Top 10 Rules for Romping Off-leash

Best Tips for Hiking with your Dog

Packing Tricks for Dog Trips

"If you can resist treating a rich friend better than a poor friend,
If you can face the world without lies and deceit,
If you can say honestly that deep in your heart you have no prejudice against creed, color, religion or politics,
Then, my friend, you are almost as good as your dog."

———

Unknown Author

PAWS ON THE BUS, MONORAIL & CITY CENTER

Can I take my dog on the Metro city bus?

Pets are allowed on city busses. That doesn't mean your dog will want to go for a ride. How well behaved is your dog? Even the best-trained dog can have a snarly day if s/he isn't feeling well. The transit operator, at his or her discretion, may not allow you to board with your pet if there is a concern for the safety or comfort of your fellow passengers. Get to know your dog's signals and decide if your dog is socialized enough and feeling well enough to ride the bus. If so, tighten up on the leash as you board and lets' go!

Dogs may ride at the discretion of the operator under these guidelines:

- Drivers may refuse to transport a person and their dog if they already have another dog onboard.

- Drivers may refuse to transport a dog if it is creating a hazard or disturbance.

- Drivers may request the removal of a dog from the coach if it creates a hazard or disturbance.

- All dogs that are not service animals must be on leash.

- Dogs are not allowed to occupy seats; they must remain either on the floor or sit on their owners lap.

- Small dogs who remain on their owner's lap ride for free. All other dogs pay the base fare (or reduced fare) paid by the customer accompanying the dog. No zone fare is charged and transfers are to be issued upon request.

Note: Animals other than dogs are not allowed on the coach unless they are in a container or carrier. Fare is not required.

Can I take my service dog or service-dog-in-training on the local bus?

Drivers are required to permit any customer with a service animal to ride King County Metro buses. This includes animals-in-training accompanied by a trainer or person with a disability.

Service animals for persons with disabilities ride for free. No permit is required, but the driver may ask if your animal is a service animal to determine if a fare is appropriate.

Service animals must remain on the floor without blocking the aisle or on their owner's lap. If this is not an option, the service animal may occupy a seat provided one is available.

If the service animal's behavior threatens the safety of the driver or other passengers the customer and their service animal may be asked to leave the bus.

Are dogs allowed on the Monorail?

Dogs are allowed as long as they are well-behaved and on a leash. On busy/crowded days, it is possible that the owner may be asked to hold their dog in their lap.

Are dogs allowed in the Seattle center?

The Seattle Center is the former grounds of the 1962 World Fair, which has been converted into a 72-acre urban park. It includes the famous Space Needle, as well as a large fountain area. Leashed dogs are allowed to walk around in the outdoor parts, but cannot enter the buildings.

Do you allow pets at Pike Place Market?

Pets are not allowed in Market buildings, including the Main Arcade. Only trained service animals are permitted within Market buildings.

Does the Seattle great wheel allow pets?

I've never seen a dog on a Ferris wheel. It makes me wonder if dogs get airsick, or motion sickness. If I were a dog and suddenly found myself high in the sky, I'd flip out. Keep that in mind. Service animals are allowed on board but that doesn't mean your service dog will want to go. Please notify the ticket booth if you have a service animal, and be prepared to answer service animal questions as allowed by Federal and State law.

DOG PARKS
DO'S AND DON'TS

Some days at dog parks are like heaven with happy dogs romping and getting along with one another. Some days, you find yourself mixed in with creepy dog owners and dogs from hell. Following are some basic guidelines that should be taken into consideration when bringing your dog to a dog park. Remember this – if you don't feel safe, leave!

Be sure to take your dog's temperament into consideration and don't assume s/he's having a good time – watch your dog's demeanor and make an informed judgment about how happy s/he is to be there. Some dogs will have no desire to play, yet will love to sniff all the bushes and trees; other dogs will be thrilled to race another dog from one end of the park to the other. Both of these dogs can benefit from the dog park – they just enjoy it in different ways.

If you take the time to be an informed dog owner, you will be able to judge for yourself if the situation you and your dog are in is a good situation – so, have fun at the dog park and get yourself a pooper scooper!

Don't

- Bring a dog that is under 4 months of age
- Take sensitive dogs to an enclosed dog park where there are more than 2 dogs per every 20 square yards of space
- Take your dog to a dog park if s/he is uncomfortable -- take your dog to a place that s/he enjoys
- Bring or use treats and toys when other dogs are nearby
- Allow dogs to form loose packs
- Allow a dog to bully another
- Ever let your dog off-leash in an un-fenced dog park if he/she is not responsive to your verbal commands
- Worry if some dogs don't play with other dogs in a dog park
- Bring intact males or females in estrus to a dog park
- Spend your time talking on a cell phone - you must supervise your dog at all times and be able to give your dog your full attention

Do

- Consult your veterinarian about your dog's overall health before going to a dog park
- Make sure your dog is up-to-date on his/her vaccinations
- Observe the dogs in the dog park to see if there are any potential health or behavior problems

- Clean up after your dog

- Supervise dogs when they are playing and interrupt any rough play

- Be willing to leave a dog park if you feel that your dog is either being a bully, the play is getting too rough or your dog is just not having fun

- Check to be sure there aren't a large number of intact males at the park

- Make sure your young dog is not being bullied or learning bad manners from the other dogs

- Be cautious about taking advice from other park patrons who are not dog professionals

- Check to see if there is a knowledgeable human on staff to supervise the park

"My Labrador retriever had a nervous breakdown. I kept throwing him a boomerang."

———

Nick Arnette

TOP 10
RULES FOR ROMPING OFF-LEASH

1. Respect other park visitors by keeping your dog from jumping on, or interfering with, other people and their dogs. Off-leash does not mean out of control.

2. You are liable for damage or injury inflicted by your dog(s) (SMC 18.12.080).

   • You must be in control of your dog(s) at all times (SMC 18.12.080).

   • You must muzzle dogs that exhibit dangerous or aggressive behavior; biting, fighting, and excessive barking are not allowed (SMC 9.25.024).

3. You must leash your dog when it is outside the off-leash area; you must carry a leash for each dog while you are inside the off-leash area (SMC 9.25.084 and 12.18.080).

4. You are required by law to pick up your dog's feces and to properly dispose of it in the trashcans located throughout the area.

- You must clean up after your dog(s) and deposit feces in the containers at the site, and you must visibly carry scoop equipment (SMC 9.25.082 and 18.12.080).

5. You must closely supervise young children.

6. Bring food into off-leash areas at your own risk.

7. Leave bicycles outside off-leash area.

8. Unattended dogs are not allowed in off-leash areas. Owners who see unattended dogs or other rule violations should call Animal Control at 206-386-7387, extension

- If you're female dog and you're in heat, you are not allowed in off-leash areas (SMC 9.25.084).

- If you're a puppy younger than four months of age, you are not allowed in off-leash areas.

9. To come and play in off-leash areas, you need to be licensed and vaccinated (SMC 9.25.080 and 12.18.080).

10. If you wear a pinch or choke collar, ask your human to remove it when you come into off-leash areas.

BEST TIPS FOR
HIKING WITH YOUR DOG

There's no better company on the hiking trail than your dog—
man's best friend also makes for man's best hiking companion. But
preparing your dog for hiking requires some pre-hike care to ensure
that your dog enjoys the hike safely. Before you and your furry friend
hit the trails, be sure to check off this list of must-dos:

Foot Care

All dogs are born with front dewclaws, and many have rear dewclaws.
This fifth digit on the inside of the leg is prone to tearing; an option
is to have it removed by a veterinarian within a few days after birth.

Nails should be comfortably short without sacrificing traction.
Even dogs that are active enough outdoors to keep their nails naturally
worn need to have their nails trimmed. Ask a groomer or a vet about
the proper use of nail clippers and files.

Feet: Dog footpads get tough (light sandpaper texture) from walks and runs on pavement, sand, and rocks. They should wear booties to alleviate tenderness and protect footpads from cuts on ice and sharp rocks.

Be careful of extreme cold and extreme heat, hot ground, and especially blacktop on hot days if road walking. This can easily hurt a dog's paws. Remember if it is 100°F out, the pavement temperature can be much hotter than that.

Dog owners swear by Musher's Secret for those knarly weather hiking days. This easy-to-apply all-natural wax-based cream protects paws from harsh surfaces. Protect paws from sand, hot pavement, ice and salt with all natural 100 percent wax-based cream. When applied to pads and between toes, dries in seconds to form a semi-permeable shield. Nontoxic, non-allergenic, non-staining formula can be used weekly or as needed to prevent abrasions, burning, drying and cracking. Perfect for mushing, hunting, walking or before any outdoor activity. Acts as an invisible boot to prevent potential paw problems.

Health Care

Your dog should be current on all vaccinations (DHLP-P, rabies, and a vaccination against Lyme disease are advisable). Veterinarians will now customize a vaccine just for your dog, taking into account age and lifestyle. If you live in rattlesnake country, ask the vet about the vaccine against rattlesnake venom.

Heartworm: Mosquitoes carry this parasite. Consult your vet about heartworm preventive medication.

West Nile Virus: Mosquitoes carry this virus. No vaccine or specific treatment exists, but consult your vet if you'd like more information.

Fleas and Ticks: Dogs can get tapeworms by swallowing fleas that carry disease. The arsenal of flea and tick products on the market is bigger than ever.

Grooming

During summer, trim (don't shave) long coats, particularly under the belly and behind the legs. Don't forget to shave the hair between their toes to prevent the bushy spikelets of foxtail grass from going undetected and leading to infections. In winter, less hair between the toes prevents icicles around the pads and frostbite.

Here is another tip for when your dog rolls in that fish carcass laying by the river or gets sprayed by a skunk.

Earth Friendly Products Petastic Skunk Odor Remover is the Holy Grail of pee-stink eliminators. This Professional Strength Bio-Enzymatic formula is guaranteed to virtually eliminate any stain and odor from urine, feces, vomit, and other organic stains. This non-toxic formula also discourages pets' attraction to stained areas by making odors disappear while removing stains from carpeting, rugs or upholstery.

On or Off leash?

Hiking with an excited dog pulling on your leash is hard on your arm but pacing yourself and the dog early on makes for a better ending to the hike depending on the distance you want to travel. Leashing your dog is the respectful thing to do in case there are other people around—some people may not like dogs and children certainly don't want to be bumped off the trail by a large, rambunctious dog. Too many places that have already banned dogs, and if dog owners do not act responsibly and respectfully, then we will lose many of the remaining areas where we are currently allowed.

The type of leash you carry depends on you and your dog's preferences and pet stores abound with leashes. Good pet owners know that the collar you attach the leash to, is just as important. The PetSafe Easy Walk Harness is one of the favorite harnesses of dog owners.

Food & Water on the Trail

Make sure to bring food and water on a hike not just for yourself but for fido, too. For multi-day hikes, puppy food is higher in calories and makes a great dog food on the trail. If you are just day hiking remember that your dog needs to snack to keep up his/her energy – just like you do. Take some high calorie dog treats such as Newman's Own Organics New Zealand Ranch Style Dog Treats

Treat bags are a necessity on the trail and for training. Attach a treat bag to your belt or outside your pack for easy access to call your dog or give a reward. Canine Equipment Carry-all Treat Bags offers one of the best!

Water isn't always available when your dog's panting and looking at you as if to say, "I'm dying of thirst!" After letting my dog drink one too many times from my own water bottle, I broke down and purchased one for him. This is the best! H2O4K9 Dog Water Bottle and Travel Bowl.

If you want to train your dog to carry their own food and water and supplies, the Kygen 2502 Dog Backpack is the best on the market. Break him/her in slowly to the pack, increasing mileage and weight and watching for signs of chafing if you plan to do multi-day hikes with your dog..

Reading Signals

How do you tackle crossing bodies of water? When fording a swift river, hold onto the dog's collar on the downstream side so that s/he won't get swept downstream and you won't throw him/her off-balance.

What else is good to know about hiking with a dog? Hiking with a dog can be very individual; you will find your own tricks and learn how to read your dog's expressions if you pay attention. Do you know when your dog is getting thirsty? While training my puppy to accompany me on hikes, she would nudge the water bottle in my hand as a signal to give her a squirt when she got thirsty. Then she would plop down on the trail and refuse to budge towards the end of the hike. Rest and treat time. Her signals were so obvious that I could not ignore them.

Getting Conditioned for Longer Hikes

Get started by increasing the length of your day hikes and move up to overnight hikes. As you go, you will find that both of you have built up the tolerance, mileage, and endurance. Teach your dog to sit-stay when you stop to rest rather than let him/her run around. When you remove your pack, signal your dog to take a snooze. The more you hike together, the more your dog will pick up on your signals.

PACKING TRICKS
FOR DOG TRIPS

Traveling with a dog used to be as archaic as traveling with small children in the days before seatbelt laws when kids would crawl at will across seats and kick the driver in the face on her way to the passenger seat. Kids sat on mom's lap in the front seat while dad drove. Kids also hunkered down in the back of pickup trucks exposed to wind and gravel blow back. Kids slept sprawled out on a blanket the full length of the seat. Dogs were no different – leaping at will across seats or sniffing the wind from the back of a bouncing pick up. A blanket on the car seat and a cracked window is all we used to need for the dog.

Not much has changed for many dog owners. For some owners, that still works.

Wherever we go, we inevitably see a dog nose poking out the driver's side window or sitting in the passenger seat, panting breath fogging the glass. Rest stops along freeways you'll see dogs on leash, their owners stretching their legs and hoping the dog will do its business before getting back in the car. Some hard and awkward bowl of water gets laid out on the grass or hot cement. Often, the dog will be left in the car overnight while the owners sleep in a hotel.

Times have changed for other dog owners who are savvy about keeping their canine and their car interior in better shape through the miles of urban and vacation travel.

Traveling by Car

No matter how big or small your dog is, you probably have the car transportation issue settled.

Safest for all concerned is the crate transport. Get your dog used to the crate well before you travel. The size of the crate depends on the size of your dog. Consult your local pet store for more information.

Dog Entertainment in Confinement

Forget the video player drop down or listening to the radio, give fido something to crew on and that may be all the stimulus/he needs for awhile on the road trip or in a hotel. A good chew toy can prevent many behavioral issues like destructive chewing or excessive vocalization from boredom or anxiety.

For some reason dogs like peanut butter. And, like humans, they like cold treats on hot days. Stick a few Kongs that have been stuffed with your dog's favorite treats and frozen overnight into your cooler before you leave home.

The KONG Classic has been the gold standard of dog toys for over 36 years. Stuffing healthy treats into a KONG keeps dogs happily working and out of trouble for long periods of time.

One person I know makes a combination of kibble and peanut butter.

The Kong keeps her dog occupied for hours in the car and because it's frozen, it lasts even longer and he spends forever licking and biting at the Kong to get the goodies out. Dogs need something to do with their mouths. They use their muzzles like we use our hands. A stuffed Kong can prevent so many behavioral issues like destructive chewing or excessive vocalization from boredom or anxiety.

Food and Water on the Road

Forget packing a hard bowl. Collapsible bowls are so much easier to use for dry food and water that your traveling dog will love them. Kygen 2482 Port-a-Bowl is collapsible, clean and the best on the pet travel market.

Dogs have their own ideas of what they like to eat and often frustrate their human companions with fussy eating habits. While traveling, dry food is easier to pack but may not be initially accepted by your pooch. Before you hit the road, try a few different types of dry food and see how your dog accepts the choice. Here are two of the best selling, especially for dogs with diet-related allergies and dry skin.

- Castor & Pollux Organix Adult Canine Formula Dry Dog Food
- Taste of the Wild Dry Dog Food, HiPrairie Canine Formula with Roasted Bison & Venison

Hotel, Cruise Ships & Host Homes

Accidents happen from puppyhood to old age – especially when traveling. Good travelers carry something to clean up after their dogs. Rocco & Roxie Enzyme formula odor and stain remover will make you and your host happy in case of an accident.

I was talking with a couple on a cruise ship, traveling with their seeing eye dogs and asked them the question they receive the most – where does your dog pee on a cruise ship? They responded that they were responsible for their dog's eliminations and so they took puppy pads and a collapsible box that they kept on the balcony of their room. A week before each cruise, they re-train the dogs to eliminate on cue and in the box. They haven't have any accidents on a cruise ship or while traveling.

Here is what they packed:

- Super Absorbent Training Pads
- A Training Pad Holder

Don't forget you Dog bed or dog's favorite blanket. Travel is stressful. Sleeping in a familiar scent makes a dog more relaxed.

GO!

Best Dog Trainers and Agility Training Fun

Top 10 Doggie Day Spas

Top 7 Doggie Day Cares

Top Dog Vets

Top 10 Dog-Friendly Restaurants

Top 12 Dog Parks On & Off Leash

Best Doggon Beach Parks

Best Doggie Diversions
(Meet-Ups, Shopping, Movies, Wineries, Breweries)

Best Local Hikes for Dogs

Hiking with your Dog in State and National Parks
Q & A

"If your dog doesn't like someone,
you probably shouldn't either."

———

Unknown Author

BEST DOG TRAINERS AND AGILITY TRAINING FUN

My friend couldn't stand her husband's new puppy. Used to being the alpha in the family, she stared right into the pup's eyes and realized that the little creature was destined to become the Queen. The huge pup was unruly, full of energy, and no match for an older retired man on the walking trails nearby. Chewing up every shoe on the floor and anything else within reach of her mouth, my friend knew that her house was destined for ruin unless she got her hubby to take the pup to learn some better behaviors. So they went to Puppy Manners the premier school in Woodinville for puppy initial training and older dog remedial training. The Puppy Manners Ranch Board and Train program fits the bill for anyone who wants to have someone work with their dog while they are away on vacation or medical leave, or just want someone else to take over the puppy love for a few weeks. Two weeks after my friends took their Bernese Mountain pup, the staff worked with them alongside their dog, to practice newly learned behaviors.

A well-behaved dog is a must for owners today. Not only will some obedience training help tragic prevent accidents in dog parks and public places, it will make your home feel like YOUR home. Here are some of the best training centers around according to reviews on Yelp and other sites.

Seattle/Eastside Puppy Manners

425.482.1057
info@puppymanners.com
http://www.puppymanners.com

SEATTLE

Paws for Training

4015 Stone Way N, Seattle 98103
http://www.paws4training.com

Services Offered:
- Puppy Kindergarten Socialization
- Beginning Agility and K9 Good Citizen
- Reactive Dog
- Introducing your dog to your baby

Private in home classes and behavior consultations are available upon request

K-9 Fun Zone

25 Nickerson St., Seattle, WA 98109
http://www.k9funzoneseattle.com/fun-agility.html

For the cold rainy days, K-9 Fun Zone private indoor dog park is the perfect place for you and your pooch to play. The Main attraction: Their pawesome agility course. This agility course is perfect to satisfy and wear your dog out.

Services Offered:
- Agility based classes
- Puppy & Adult Manners
- Reactive Rover
- Pet First Aid Weekend Workshop

Nitro K-9

7542 Roosevelt Way Northeast, Seattle, WA 98115
(206) 412-9979
http://nitrocanine.com/site/index.php?main_page

The Seattle based facility specializes in Anxiety and Aggression in K-9's. One thing that sticks this dog training out from the rest is their Non Food Based training. Instead they, "…exchange love and praise for behavior and specific leash techniques.

Services Offered:
- The Mini Heroes Training Programs
- The Aggression Stopper
- The Emotional Support Training Program
- Canine Security & Personal Protection Program
- Board & Train Program

Kat Albrecht Pet Detective

PO Box 3085 Federal Way, WA 98063-3085
http://www.katalbrecht.com/training.php

If you are seeking a volunteer or professional career for you and your Dog, Kat Albrecht is your perfect fit. Kat is the founder of Missing Pet Partnership, a national nonprofit working to develop community-based lost pet services. This former police officer now trains dogs to act in emergency situations to find lost pets.

Services Offered:
- 10-week Pet Detective "MAR" course (Missing Animal Response)
- 6-week "Dog Rescue" or "Cat Rescue" Course
- 3-Hour "Lost Pet Recovery for Pet Professionals" Webinar
- 2-Hour "Creative Captures" Webinar

Ahimsa Dog Training

Ahimsa Dog Training, LLC
925 NW 49th Street, Suite C Seattle, WA 98107
(206) 364-4072
http://ahimsadogtraining.com

Ahimsa Dog Training classes target dogs that are dealing with: aggression, dogs needing work on manners, and little puppies.

Services Offered:
- Puppy Element Primary School
- Puppy Jr. High
- Basic Dog Manners
- Intermediate/Advanced Dog Manners
- Control Unleashed
- Fear and Aggression 101
- Growly Dog
- BAT Clinic for Reactive Dogs

Companion Animal Solutions

800-920-2858 • 206-953-0703
info@companionanimalsolutions.com
http://www.companionanimalsolutions.com

Classes are held at the K9 Fun Zone: 25 Nickerson Street Seattle, WA 98109 and/or safe, outdoor locations in Seattle.

Serving Seattle, Tacoma, Everett, Olympia and surrounding areas.

Services Offered:
- Fun-gility class
- Reactive Rover class
- Puppy playgroups
- In Home Dog Training
- Help for Behavioral Issues
- Dog-Training Classes

EAST SIDE

No Worries 4 pets

4625 149th Ave SE Bellevue, WA, 98006
425.444.9322
http://www.noworries4pets.com

Services offered:
- Daytime Pet Sitting Visits
- Overnight Pet & House Sitting
- Hotel Pet Sitting
- In-Home Cage Free Boarding
- Dog Walking
- Day Care

- Dog Park Adventures
- Small Dog Playdates
- Puppy Play and Socializing
- Doggie Play School™
- Private Training
- New Dog Consulting
- Pet PA Express™
- Pet Taxi
- Pet Supply Delivery

Diane Rich Dog Training

P.O. Box 2872 Kirkland, WA 98083
(425) 576-1146
http://www.spokesdog.com

Services Offered:
- Puppy to senior training
- Training for Therapy Pets
- Group training – socialization, etc

Dog Works Ranch

25827 NE 80th ST Redmond, WA 98053
425-643-2516
http://www.dogworksranch.com

Services Offered:
- 5 acres of romping range for dog boarding
- shuttle to play groups
- board and train

NW Dog Pros

13229 112th Ave NE, Kirkland, Wa 98034
(360) 981-3294
shttp://www.nwdogpro.com

Classes Offered:
- Pet partners Puppy manners
- Agility training SAR Training

Services Offered:
- 5 acres of romping range for dog boarding
- shuttle to play groups
- board and train

TOP 10
DOGGIE DAY SPAS

Drop off your dog on your way to work or before you go shopping on Saturday and pamper your pet for a few hours of grooming, fur styling, at one of these top rated spas for dogs. (Ratings derived from Yelp and other sites.) If you would rather do-it-yourself, a few places offer a place and tools to shape up your canine companion.

SEATTLE

Just Around the Corner Dog Grooming & Boutique

619 Queen Anne N. Seattle, WA 98109
206.453.4323
http://www.jatcgrooming.com

Bark in Style

4411 Wallingford Ave. N. Seattle, WA 98103
(206) 547-9211
http://barkinstyle.fullslate.com

Great Dog

11333 Roosevelt Way NE Seattle, WA 98125
206-850-2529
http://www.gogreatdog.com

Posh Paws Grooming Salon

64111 Roosevelt Way NE Seattle, WA 98115
(206) 257-4887
http://poshpawsseattle.com

Rex

1402 12th Ave Seattle, WA 98122
(206) 467-4440
http://www.rexseattle.com

EASTSIDE

Tesslan Dog Spa

14210 NE 20th St. Bellevue, WA 98007
(425) 747-4731
https://www.tesslandogspa.com

Tia's Doggie Spa

12305 120th Ave NE, Suite H Kirkland, WA 98034
425-820-1000
http://tiasdoggiespa.com

Ruff House Self-Service Dog Wash

8058 161st Ave NE Redmond, WA 98052
425-556-5103
http://www.ruffhousedogwash.com

Mutt N Chops Ruff Styles

22330 NE Marketplace Dr. Redmond, WA 98053
(425) 898-1312
mutt-n-chops.com

Scruff to Fluff

222 Central Way Kirkland, WA 98033
(425) 827-3144
http://www.viewmenu.com/scruff-to-fluff/menu?ref=google

TOP 7
DOGGIE DAY CARES

No one wants to leave their dog home alone for a full workday away, unless they have a need for a watch dog to guard their property. Here are a few top-rated day cares for dogs. (Ratings are derived from Yelp and other sites.)

SEATTLE

Play Doggie Day Care

2765 East Cherry St. Seattle, WA 98122
206-209-8238
http://www.playdoggiedaycare.com/Home.html

Play Doggie Day Care has four separate areas for your doggie to roam: 2 indoor and 2 outdoor (usually they separate large dogs from smaller ones). Along with their visit there is also a bath time and dogs are sent home clean.

Additional Services offered:
- Drop off/Pick up
- Walking the Dog
- Jake & Friends

Taxi Services are offered to and from play, as well as any other places you may need to get your dog. Ex: vet appt, grooming, etc.

Barking Lounge

222 Dexter Ave N Seattle, WA 98109
206 382 1600
http://www.barkinglounge.com

Voted best Dog Daycare in Seattle, the Lounge is kept very clean and hosts web cams so owners may see their dogs online while away.

Great Dog

11333 Roosevelt Way NE Seattle, WA 98125
206-850-2529
http://www.gogreatdog.com

At Great Dog, your dog will participate a safe, fun atmosphere & will enjoy getting tuckered out during the day."

Rocket Dog Care

9035 12th Avenue Northwest, Seattle, WA 98117
(206) 491-3481

EASTSIDE

Bone-A-Fide

7928 184th Street SE Snohomish, WA 98296
360-668-1756
http://www.bone-a-fide.com/dog-daycare/

Drop off and Pickup Service area:
Van service is currently available in much of Seattle and Snohomish County, including: Ballard, Queen Anne, Fremont, University District, Magnolia, Wallingford, Greenwood, Greenlake, Lake City, Northgate, Wedgewood, Ravenna, Lake Forest Park, Kenmore, Bothell, Mill Creek, Kirkland, Clearview, parts of Belltown, parts of Capitol Hill and parts of Woodinville

Scampers Daycamp for Dogs

12532 124th St. NE Kirkland, WA 98034
425-821-9100
http://www.scampersdogs.com

Dog Works Ranch LLC

25827 NE 80th ST. Redmond, WA 98053
425-643-2516
http://www.dogworksranch.com/index.php/2013-07-08-04-02-43/shuttle

Drop off and pick up service area:
Mercer Island, Bellevue, Redmond, Woodinville, Totem Lake, Duvall, and Kirkland.

TOP DOG VETS

The best veterinarian is one that you and your dog feel most comfortable with on any given day. In emergencies, you want your vet to be within a short diving distance. Here are a few of the top rated in the region according to Yelp reviews and reviews on other sites.

SEATTLE

Aurora Veterinary Hospital

8821 Aurora Ave N Seattle, WA 98103

206.525.6666

http://www.auroraveterinaryhospital.com/avh/Welcome.html

Urban Animal

1001 Broadway Ave. Suite 109 Seattle, WA
(206) 329-5337
http://urbananimalnw.com

Pet Care Center

2950 SW Avalon Way Seattle, WA 98126
(206) 935-3600
http://www.petcarecenteratlunapark.com

Companion Pet Clinic

706 NE 45th St. Seattle, WA 98105
206-257-0504
http://www.cpcseattle.com

Lake Union Veterinary Clinic

1222 Republican St. Seattle, WA 98109
(206) 467-5882
http://www.lakeunionvet.com

EASTSIDE

Crossroads Vet

15600 NE 8th ST. Bellevue, WA 98008
425-746-PETS (7387)
http://www.bellevuecrossroadsvet.com

Brookfield Veterinary Hospital

6535 E Lake Sammamish Pkwy NE Redmond, WA 98052
425-895-8888
http://www.redmondvet.com

Loyal Companion Animal Care

22330 NE Market Place Dr, Suites 113 & 115, Redmond, WA 98053
http://www.loyalcompanionanimalcare.com

Loyal Family Veterinary Hospital

677 120th Ave NE Bellevue, WA 98005
425-201-1908
http://www.loyalfamilyvet.com

Juanita Bay Veterinary Hospital

11416 98th Ave NE Kirkland, WA 98033
(425) 823 - 8411
http://juanitabayvet.com

Redmond-Kirkland Animal Hospital

7251 W Lake Sammaish Pkwy NE Redmond, WA 98052
425-882-8000
http://www.redmondkirklandveterinary.com

TOP 10
DOG FRIENDLY RESTAURANTS

Dogs are welcomed to outside seating in more and more restaurants these days. But keep in mind that managers of cafes, breweries, and places that sell and serve food, are under scrutiny by other customers and the Department of Health. An unobtrusive dog is always welcome. A hyper dog that jumps on people and tables or piddles on the floor will almost always be asked to leave. Puppies, no matter how cute, are no exception.

SEATTLE

Bongos

6501 Aurora Ave. N Seattle, WA 98103
206.420.8548
http://bongoscubancafeseattle.com

Great place to go after a romp around Greenlake.

Hours:
Sun. to Thurs. – 11 a.m. to 9 p.m. (Closed Mondays)
Fri. to Sat. – 11 a.m. to 10 p.m.

Bark! Espresso

11335 Roosevelt Way NE Seattle, WA 98125
http://www.barkespresso.com

Bark! Espresso is the first dog friendly café Located in the Pinehurst-Northgate area. You and your pup can mingle with other dog lovers at the Great Dog Lounge called the Hound Hangout.

Hours:
Sun. – 8 a.m. – 4 p.m.
Sat. – 8 a.m. - 5 p.m.
Mon. to Fri. – 7 a.m. - 5:30 p.m.

Norm's Eatery & Ale House

460 N. 36th St. Seattle, WA 98103
206-547-1417
http://normseatery.com

Norm's brings the inner dog lover to life. In this restaurant you will see doggie décor scattered throughout. They are known for the Thursday night Trivia Team competitions.

Hours:
Mon. – Thurs. – 11 a.m. to 12 a.m.
Fri. – 11 a.m. – 2 a.m.
Sat. – 8 a.m. to 2 a.m.
Sun – 8 a.m. to 12 a.m.

Bandits Bar

159 Denny Way Seattle, WA 98109
(206) 443-5447

An old western themed bar that serves Mexican food. They are known for their tamales. Dogs are welcomed as long as they are on leash.

Hours:
4 p.m. to 2 a.m.

Belltown Pub

2322 1st Ave Seattle, WA 98121
206-448-6210
http://belltownpub.com

This hot spot for hounds features a special "Pup Grub" menu. Dogs can dine alongside their human companions at (or under) the table.

Hours:
Mon. to Fri. – 11 a.m. to 2 a.m.
Sat. and Sun. – 9 a.m. to 2 a.m.

EASTSIDE

Purple Café and Wine Bar

Kirkland: 323 Park Place Center Kirkland, WA 98033
Bellevue: 430 106th Ave NE Bellevue, WA 98004

Dogs welcomed in outdoor dining area.

Olive You and the Tervelli Ultralounge

89 Kirkland Avenue Kirkland, Washington 98033

520 Bar & Grill

10146 Main Street Bellevue, WA 98004
http://520barandgrill.com

Paddy Coyne's

Bellevue: 700 Bellevue Way NE Suite 100 Bellevue, WA 98004
Seattle: 1190 Thomas St. Seattle, WA 98109
http://www.paddycoynes.net

Stone House

16244 Cleveland St. Redmond, WA 98052
http://stonehouseredmond.com

"Man is a dog's ideal of what God should be."

———

Holbrook Jackso

TOP 12
DOG PARKS ON & OFF LEASH

There is nothing more fun than seeing your dog romp off leash, tongue hanging out, a big smile on his or her face, tail wagging freely in the wind. Dogs love to run with a pack. Their owners love to meet up, too. Fortunately, Seattle and the east side have so many wonderful parks to choose from that dog owners have the luxury of frequenting the local park or roaming a little further afield. Why be a creature of habit? Go exploring!

If its too rainy and you don't care to wipe the mud off your shoes before you get back in the car after a romp in a park, consider an outing to the K9 Fun Zone. There is lots of fun for you and your canine companion in a dry indoor environment.

K9 Fun Zone: Private Indoor Dog Park

25 Nickerson St. Seattle, WA 98109
206-281-5095
http://www.k9funzoneseattle.com

SEATTLE

Denny Park

100 Dexter Ave. N Seattle, WA 98109
http://www.seattle.gov/parks/offleash_detail.asp?id=309

This off-leash area of .105 acres is located at 100 Dexter Avenue North in the north-central sector of Denny Park, off John Street. Denny Park was created in 1883 and is the City's oldest park; influenced by the Olmsted Plan. The park has large trees and is carefully landscaped with grass and an assortment of plantings. There is a children's play area, benches and recently installed lighting. The off-leash area is temporary until a permanent site is located in the South Lake Union neighborhood. This park and the off-leash area is wheelchair accessible. There is a 4' tall fence that encloses the off-leash area and double gates at the entrance to ensure your dog's safety. Surfacing in the off-leash area is granolithic gravel.

Magnuson Park

7400 Sand Point Way NE Seattle, WA 98115
http://www.seattle.gov/parks/offleash_detail.asp?id=398

Magnuson Park's off-leash area is by far the largest, most popular and most widely used off-leash area in Seattle. The Magnuson off-leash area contains 9 acres. It is a place where city hounds can romp with buddies in Seattle's biggest fully-fenced back yard for canines. This off-leash area is the only one inside city limits with water access (Lake Washington's freshwater shoreline). The site has a large, generally flat play area, a winding trail with several open areas and changes of scenery along the way, and it gives dog owners and their dogs of all ages plenty of space to "work out". Most of the trail is compact gravel and is wheelchair accessible. This off-leash area has a small and shy dog area within the larger dog park. Fencing and signs were installed in coordination with the Magnuson Off Leash Area Group (MOLG). The small/shy dog area is located just to the south of the main entrance kiosk, accessible from NE 74th street.

Dr. Jose Rival Park

1008 12th Ave S. Seattle, WA 98144
http://www.seattle.gov/parks/offleash_detail.asp?id=433

This off-leash area is located just south of downtown on the north end of Beacon Hill. It is currently 4 acres and offers spectacular views of Puget Sound looking west and to the Seattle Downtown skyline looking north. The park was recently renovated after the Department of Transportation constructed a bicycle path connecting to the Mountains to Sound Greenway. There is water available for dogs to drink. The fenced areas is accessed from a long set of stairs at the north end of the Park. It is ADA accessible from the bicycle trail. A trail runs through the middle of the off-leash area which is compacted gravel and follows rolling contours.

Northacres Park

12718 1st Ave. NE Seattle, WA 98125
http://www.seattle.gov/parks/offleash_detail.asp?id=361

Consisting of .7 acres off leash area, Northacres Park has numerous trees, trails, and open area for your dog to roam. The off leash area is in the NE corner of the park.

Westcrest Dog Park

800 SW Henderson St. Seattle, WA
http://www.seattle.gov/parks/offleash_detail.asp?id=468

Westcrest Park is located on a hill above and west of Boeing Field in southwest Seattle. It contains approximately 4 acres and features open spaces and paths, a doggie drinking fountain, shade, trees and lots of open space. For people, the off-leash area provides benches, chairs, and a shady place to relax. Restrooms, play areas and picnic areas are nearby. Improvements include a parking lot, fencing, shelters and lighting. Parking is available in the Westcrest parking lot, which is located approximately 150 yards south of the off-leash area. Dogs need to be leashed when walking between the parking lot and the off-leash area. A special, separated area for small and shy dogs is located on the southwest side of the main off-leash area.

EASTSIDE

If you would like to meet-up with other dog owners, check out the Kirkland Dog Off-leash Group at *http://www.kdog.org*.

Jasper's Dog Park (Off leash access)

11225 NE 120th St. Kirkland WA, 98034
Park Rules: *http://www.kdog.org/Home/Rules*

This park offers a huge area for your dogs to run, run, run and run more. The park also sports a nice tree area on top of the hill which provides shade and another run area for your dogs to play keep away. Its well thought out and offers a small dog area separate from the big dogs area to keep the little ones from getting rolled over. There is also a small agility course set up at the top left of the hill with two jumps, a ramp, and a fake hollow log to run through.

Medina Park (Off leash access)

8000 NE 12th ST. Medina, WA 98039

This is a great dog park right in the heart of Medina. For half of the year the entire park is entirely off-leash (the wetter half). And for the other half of the year, they limit the off leash area to the East half of the park. Not to fear though, you can still take your dog to the West side of the park - you just have to keep him/her on a leash at that point. This is probably because during those warmer months, the park is used a lot by families with small children and occasionally also as a meeting place for kids soccer teams and such. There are two big ponds here separated by a small stream. There's even a "launching area" on the Southern pond so that dogs and swim and fetch to their heart's content. This pond is popular with the dogs in the summer time when it gets warmer and they can all use a refreshing dip. And there are a couple of watering bowls, complete with water hose nearby, strategically placed throughout the park. Nice walking trail all around the park. Plenty of free poop-scoop bags with disposal cans all throughout the park.

Luther Burbank (Off leash access)

2040 84th Ave SE
Mercer Island, WA
http://parkstrails.myparksandrecreation.com/details.aspx?pid=389

The north end of Luther Bank Park offers a fenced off-leash dog area. This space, bordered on one end by shoreline is a great place to let the dogs run, play, and swim. It is a short walk from the north parking lot. City of Mercer Island Code states that dogs may be off-leash but under control by using voice or signal commands within the fenced area.

Marymoor Park AKA "Doggy Disneyland" (Off leash access)

40 Acres of off leash dog park.
6046 W. Lake Sammaish Parkway NE Redmond, WA
http://www.soda.org/marymoor-dog-park/about-marymoor/

Covering 40 acres, Marymoor Dog Park includes fields, woods and a river, with well maintained access beaches, paths, walkways and bridges. Over six miles of looping trails offer a variety of dog walking opportunities. Five river access points are available for dogs that like to swim and water retrieve. Acres of natural fields are available for dog romping, fetching and exploring. It is a myth that "dog parks are just for for dogs." Rather, Marymoor Dog Park provides recreation for PEOPLE – over 800,000 visitations of people with their canine companions are made to Marymoor Dog Park each year, making it one of the most popular destinations for regional recreation! Note: There is a $1 parking fee.

Robinswood Park – Off leash Dog Corral

2430 148th Ave SE Bellevue, WA 98007
http://parkstrails.myparksandrecreation.com/Details.aspx?pid=25

This is a great place to take your dog if you think he/she might take off without a leash. There are actually two dog parks here and one of them has a gated partition. The larger dogs tend to stay at the area closest to 148th and the smaller dogs tend to be at the area at the back of the park by the tennis courts (away from 148th). The small dog area has a gated partition to separate dogs if needed. With 3 areas, you're almost guaranteed to have a safe area for your dog.

Kelsey Creek Farm Park (Dogs must be on leash)

410 130th Pl SE Bellevue, WA
http://parkstrails.myparksandrecreation.com/Details.aspx?pid=23

150 acres of forest, meadows and wetlands located in the heart of Bellevue offer a glimpse of this city's rural past. The farm's two historic barns sit prominently on the crest of a hill, overlooking the shallow valleys to each side. Farm animals are out in the pastures or yards daily. Come by and see them! They are available for viewing daily from 9 a.m. to 3:30 p.m., 365 days/year, including weekends and holidays. There is no formal entrance fee; however, they welcome and appreciate your donations. When visiting Kelsey Creek Farm, all dogs and other pets must on a leash at all times. Out of respect to the farm animals' health and wellbeing, all pets are strictly prohibited from the area surrounding the barns (the barnyard).

Bellevue Downtown Park (Dogs must be on leash)

10201 NE fourth St.
http://www.ci.bellevue.wa.us/downtown_park_and_rose_garden.htm

An approximately 21-acre oasis of green in the heart of Bellevue defines this elegant centerpiece of the Bellevue Parks System. A one-half mile promenade, bordered by a double row of shade trees, and a stepped canal, brings one to the 240-foot wide waterfall that cascades into a reflecting pond. A ten-acre lawn area invites one to pause for a picnic with Bellevue's skyline and Mount Rainier in the background. The park's delightful play area and formal gardens add to family enjoyment and serve as a backdrop for community events.

"Buy a pup and your money will buy love unflinching."

———

Rudyard Kipling

BEST DOGGON BEACH PARKS

There is nothing more fun than Seattle and the east side are full of shorelines crowded with houses along the many lakes and low banks of the Salish Sea. However, city planners have left some room for public access. My favorite place to walk is along Alki Beach on the west side of Seattle. Although pets aren't allowed on the beach at Alki Beach, there's a 2.5 mile boardwalk where you can take your pet for a fun jaunt along the beachside. Loads of roller skaters and bicyclists cruise that stretch so if your dog want to bark, nip or chase out wheeled human friends, its best to keep them on a short leash.

Most beach areas are closed to dogs during the late spring through summer months but for the rest of the year – its yours! Here are the local favorites.

SEATTLE

Plymouth Pillars Dog Park

Boren Ave & Pike St
http://www.seattle.gov/parks/park_detail.asp?ID=4000

Located at the base of Capitol Hill on the Pike-Pine corridor, Plymouth Pillars Park features a close-up panoramic view of urban center of Seattle. The newly renovated park features a dog off-leash area, benches, a pedestrian corridor and public art. Open 6 a.m. to 10 p.m.

Genesee Dog Park

4316 S Genesee St.
http://www.seattle.gov/parks/park_detail.asp?ID=409

Genesee Park and Playfield is a broad, rough meadow that stretches for about 5 blocks north from Genesee Street to Stan Sayres Memorial Park on Lake Washington Boulevard. Genesee also has a fully fenced 2 1/2 acres off-leash area with double gates, a doggie drinking fountain and a kiosk for community notices. Best of all – its open from 4 a.m. to 11 p.m.!

Golden Gardens

8498 Seaview Pl NW
http://www.seattle.gov/parks/offleash_detail.asp?id=243

Who doesn't love Golden Gardens? Great beach volleyball and great beach! Golden Gardens also has a one-acre off-leash area located in the upper northern portion of the park and is a popular destination for dogs. The area includes a wide-open space covered in wood chips for playing and running. Trees are scattered throughout the off-leash area. Tables, benches and a small covered area offer places to rest and protection on rainy days. Parking and a restroom are nearby.

EASTSIDE

Dogs are not allowed at beach parks from June 1 to September 15.

Juanita Beach Park

9703 NE Juanita Dr. Kirkland, WA 98034
http://parksofkirkland.com/juanita-beach-park/

This park had/has the reputation of being the biggest beach in Kirkland (as far as sand-footage goes!) but that can also mean crowds. Typically seen at this safe and family-friendly park, are friendly locals with dogs on leash. Lots of water views and no a sunny day, sitting on the dock with your dog is a pleasant way to pass the time.

Waverly Beach Park

633 Waverly Way Kirkland, WA 98033
http://parksofkirkland.com/waverly-beach-park/

This park has some of the best views of Seattle and it feels like you are in your own private park with over 490 feet of waterfront beach to enjoy. Lots of locals walking their dogs here in the evenings and weekends. Stroll down to the beach on a wide path and enjoy a lookout over the lake with a park bench waiting just for you. It's peaceful, calm and serene. This may be one of the best places in Kirkland. From here, head south along the waterfront with a wide grassy area to the left and the waterfront to the right. To the left of the beach is a large grassy field perfect for running with the dog.

Houghton Beach Park

5811 Lake Washington Blvd, Kirkland, WA
http://parksofkirkland.com/houghton-beach-park/

This park has 900 lineal feet of waterfront and the park has many different sections to fully take advantage of all the aspects of enjoying the beach. If you like kayaking or canoeing with your dog, Houghton Beach Park Non-Motorized Boat Launch is a perfect launch point.

Idylwood Beach Park

3650 W. Lake Sammamish Redmond, WA 98052
http://www.ci.redmond.wa.us/cms/one.aspx?portalId=169&pageId=4105

Located on the shores of picturesque Lake Sammamish, Idylwood features a swimming beach, including a bathhouse and restrooms. Launch your car-top boat from the park's small ramp. Spread out and play a game in the large open space or explore Idylwood's playground area. Picnic shelters and picnic tables complete the picture for a perfect get-together. You will find plenty of parking here, as well.

"I would look at a dog and when our eyes met, I realized that the dog and all creatures are my family. They're like you and me."

———

Ziggy Marley

BEST DOGGIE DIVERSIONS
(MEET-UPS, SHOPPING, MOVIES, WINERIES, BREWERIES)

Lets face it – dogs are the best therapeutic friends available. They're happy to see you, listen without talking back, don't offer stupid advice or tell you to jump off a cliff, sympathize with you when your emotions shift into a downward spiral on a bad day, and drag you out the door when you feel least up to going anywhere. After all, you usually take your dog outside to poop and take a daily walk (or I hope you do). Like you, dogs crave stimulus with their own kind and love to get out among the pack. No one is going to let the dogs out but you and you must go, too.

So where do you go for doggie diversions that are human-friendly and you both have opportunity to engage with others of your own kind?

How about the movies? Shopping? Play dates during doggie meet ups at local parks? Or even to a local café or brewery or winery? The Seattle-Bellevue area is getting more and more dog-friendly every year.

The wonderful thing about taking your dog on an outing is that you have the opportunity to meet other dog lovers. Dogs are an awesome conversation starter. A well-trained dog can be the perfect companion and offer easy entry into a new social crowd. An ill-behaved dog, however, can isolate the both of you from the pack. So unless you are out to socialize your puppy or on a training excursion, please make sure your dog is ready for a day out in public places that involve shopping malls and eating and sipping establishments. Otherwise, you may be asked to leave and ruin it for the dog-lovers who follow.

Here are the best places to look when trying to decide where to go for a dog-diversion day.

Seattle Meet-ups

Doggone Seattle is the best place to look for friendly and fun outings that change from month to month. Dog Gone Seattle is a resource for dog owners providing information on dog-friendly establishments and activities in the greater Seattle area. The website includes restaurants, bars, cafes, retail stores, and more, and invites the community to share their favorite dog-friendly digs as well! *http://doggoneseattle.com*

If you are looking for social events for you and your dog during various holiday seasons check out the City Dog Magazine social calendar for the dog lover and furry friend. *http://www.citydogmagazine.com.*

For the ultimate hook-up for you and your dog, checkout the Seattle Active Dogs Meetup Group at: *http://www.meetup.com/seattleactivedogs/*

Seattle Active Dogs is a group that invites local dog owners to get together and connect. Outings include: Dog walks, hikes, dog parks, and restaurants allowing dogs. The meet-up page also has an area for dog owners to talk and share resources.

If you are dying for a drink but don't want to leave your dog at home, try the Yappy Hour hosted by Belltown Pub at 2322 1st Avenue in Seattle. Grab a cocktail and your Cocker Spaniel the last Wednesday of each month at the Belltown Pub. Gourmet treats are $1 off for your pup while you are offered a variety of dog themed cocktails. A great social event for dog lovers! *http://belltownpub.com*

Eastside Meet-ups

For those who dwell on the Eastside in the Bellevue and Kirkland areas and have little dogs, check out the "Bellevue Dog's under 35lb Meet-up Group" at http://www.meetup.com/bellevuedogsunder35lb-com. Don't just look them up, go! You'll be glad that you did.

For those who cannot live without their downward facing doggie routine, try taking your dog to Doga (dog yoga) located at BooBoo Bakery & Boutique in downtown Kirkland at 115 Lake St S. Doga helps doggies and their owners to relax, recalibrate, and reconnect. *http://www.booboobarkery.com/doga.html.*

Shopping

Most, if not all outdoor malls allow dogs as long as they have a leash. Nordstroms welcomes well-behaved, leashed dogs. So does the University Shopping Center and on the eastside – the Crossroads shopping center.

Despite all the hiking and outdoor recreational products REI offers, bringing your dog to REI is a no-no.

Music Festivals

Seattle, Bellevue and Woodinville host dozens of music festivals in the summer. Many are held in outdoor parks that welcome dogs. But consider your dog. Do you want to expose your dog to a crowd of people trying to either reach out and pet him or her, or shy away in fear? Is your dog well-behaved enough not to nip at a child? These crowded events can be very anxiety producing for canines. And responses vary from cowering behind you, to becoming hyper and jumping on strangers, or nipping at them.

If your dog gets kicked out of a festival, are you dumb enough to lock him or her up in a hot car and go back to sway to the music alone? It is cruel and unfair to lock a pet up, where it may experience extreme heat. You may be subjected to prosecution for animal cruelty.

If you are relying on your dog to break the ice so that you can get a conversation going with someone and get a date, you need to get out more – without your dog – and socialize without a crutch.

Only service dogs are allowed at most music festivals. There are annual music festivals such as the Birch Bay music festival north of Bellingham where dogs are allowed. You may also stumble into a music festival held in a local park during lunch or after work and bring your dog. But when it comes to Bumpershoot and Sasquatch festivals, winery and park festivals, please be considerate of your dog and others and leave your dog at home.

Movie Dates

During July and August, you can catch a movie outside with your dog several nights a week in the greater Seattle area! Grab a blanket or a couple low back chairs, pack a picnic, and go enjoy a feature film this summer! Most movies start at dusk.

All of the Outdoor Cinema features confirmed as dog-friendly are usually posted to the Dog Gone Seattle Calendar, so check that out for more details. But here's a quick summary:

Tuesdays: Outdoor Movies in Bellevue Downtown Park.

Movies are moved to South Bellevue Center in case of inclement weather. South Bellevue Center may not be dog-friendly. Each week a different charity is featured, and moviegoers are encouraged to donate specific items. Get there early for to grab a good seat. Low back chairs recommended!

Wednesdays: Outdoor Cinema at Marymoor Park

Food trucks on site each week, or bring your own food and drinks! Get there early for to grab a good seat, as this is a popular event. Seating starts at 7pm and movies are rain or shine.

Thursdays: Seattle Outdoor Movies at Magnuson Park

Food trucks are on site each week, or bring your own food and drinks! Local sponsor bars host pre-movie trivia also. Free parking north of fields. Seating starts at 7pm and movies are rain or shine.

Fridays/Saturdays: Fremont Outdoor Movies in Seattle

Held in the U-Park parking lot by Fremont Studios in Fremont Fridays or Saturdays at dusk, Jul. 12 – Aug. 23. Food trucks on site each week, and picnic style food allowed inside the event. Get there early for to grab a good seat, as this is a popular event.

Wineries

I love to sit outside with a glass of great wine and a dog's head level at my arm rest available to pet. There is something soothing about wine and dogs – a better pairing than wine and cheese most days.

Woodinville is the place to go wine tasting and listen to a little music. Almost all of the wineries are dog-friendly these days. Those that shun dogs do so usually because they have a commercial kitchen and the health inspector wouldn't like to see canine hairs floating in the air. Others have had customers complain about canine behavior. So unless your dog has gone to etiquette school and is haute- culturally behaved, please leave the dog at home and go out with your human friends instead. After all, dogs don't make good designated drivers.

If you want to know if you can bring your dog to a specific winery, the winery association has created a one-stop site just for you. *https://caninesandcabernet.wordpress.com/wineries-woodinville/*

Breweries

Heft a mug with your dog and pose for a selfie with fido at the following dog-friendly breweries but call ahead to make sure they are open on the day or evening that you want to go. If a brewery has a patio that is open, chances are your dog can sneak in without being asked for ID. For a sure bet, try one of the following favorites of Seattle's dog-lovers.

Norms

460 North 36th Street, Seattle, WA 98103
(206) 547-1417

Beveridge Place Pub

6413 California Ave SW Seattle
(206) 932-9906

Skookum Brewery

17925A 59th Ave NE at the airport in Arlington, WA
(just north of Seattle)
360-652-4917

Two Beers Brewery

4700 Ohio Avenue South, Seattle
(206) 762-0490

Schooners Exact Brewery

3901 1st Ave S
(206) 432-9734

Big Al's Brewery

9832 14th Avenue Southwest, Seattle
(206) 453-4487

No matter where you roam, the best doggie diversion is just you and your dog, running in an open field, flowers waving in the air… and you get the picture. Just go out and have fun!

BEST LOCAL HIKES FOR DOGS

For centuries, working dogs have had the run of fields and moors, mountains and beaches with their master whistling them in or using hand signals to direct the dog's movements. Few dogs are trained to such levels in our society today. You can see all manner of manners on local walking trails –from dogs running lose and jumping on strangers' children, to dogs walking obediently behind their human companion on or off leash, well trained and behaved.

Most trails call for leashes. However some are off leash. Leashing your dog is the respectful thing to do in case there are other people around—some people may not like dogs and children certainly don't want to be bumped off the trail by a large, rambunctious dog.

Hiking with an excited dog pulling on your leash is hard on your arm but pacing yourself and the dog early on makes for a better ending to the hike depending on the distance you want to travel. Too many places that have already banned dogs, and if dog owners do not act responsibly and respectfully, then we will lose many of the remaining areas where we are currently allowed.

Mount Si

North Bend
http://www.mountsi.com/mount-si-trail/

Trail is 4 miles from the parking lot.
The hike begins at the Mount Si Natural Resources Conservation Area parking lot. It climbs from a low-elevation conifer forest to the vestiges of an old burn, now becoming a new forest of firs. The fire dates back to 1910 when Mount Si burned for weeks.

At 1,600 feet (about a mile) you come to an obvious stopping place, a rocky area with a view to the valley and Interstate 90. Another obvious rest stop is reached at about 1,750 feet with benches. Snag Flats is reached in another 3/4 mile at about 2,100 feet, the only level section of trail you'll encounter. Just before Snag Flats, a short path descends to a stream, a cool place to rest on a hot day. It is about 2 1/2 more miles to Haystack Basin at about 3,900 feet (four miles total).

There are plenty of good rocky perches and benches below the Haystack. From the base of the Haystack there are views more than 3,000 feet straight down to the valley and I-90, as well as out to the Olympic Mountains and Seattle. The Haystack is a short scramble from there, and is moderate class 2/3. In the winter it can be a good mixed/ice climb.

Little Si

http://www.mountsi.com/little-si/

Hard-core hikers might think of Little Si as a desperation hike for the rare occasions when its larger counterpart, Mount Si, is under snow. And indeed, kingly Mount Si looming above is hiked year-round by mountaineers staying in shape for summer climbs. At 1,576 feet, Little Si is not a lofty peak, but it does offer imposing cliffs that climbers practice on; mountain goats are sometimes seen around it and experienced scramblers know a couple different routes to its summit. And in 1985, an army of volunteers led by Will Thompson built a new section of trail and improved sections of an old scramble route. So now hikers tackle Little Si in the winter when the wind and/or rain seem a bit much for its popular counterpart above, or simply for a change of pace. And it makes a great hike around the holidays, being close to the city and offering a chance to get out in the weather and work off some calories. Little Si is part of the Mount Si Natural Resources Conservation Area, managed by the state Department of Natural Resources and created to preserve the area's natural ecosystems. Little Si is a real mountain and on a windy day it can feel like you're miles from nowhere, especially near the summit, which is mostly bald and exposed to the elements.

Rattlesnake Ledge

http://www.wta.org/go-hiking/hikes/rattle-snake-ledge

After about a hundred feet you will be met by a "greeter" boulder, the first of many of these mossy monsters you will encounter along the lower section of the trail. As you ascend the trail and gain elevation, there will be a few places where you can look down on Rattlesnake Lake and appreciate your progress. At 1.9 miles you will reach a signed junction; though it is not signed, Rattlesnake Ledge is just to the right, about a hundred yards away. The ledge is a very exposed, large rock that has sheer cliffs, so it would be wise approach slowly if you are hiking with kids or dogs. If you wish to extend your trip you can go back to the junction where the sign points out the trail to East Peak 2.4 miles away, or the ridge traverse to Snoqualmie Park, 8.3 miles away. You can also go just a short way from the junction up to Middle Ledge and Upper Ledge, which are usually much quieter and afford more sweeping views to the northwest, where you can look down on the crowds at Rattlesnake Ledge. No pass or permit required.

Lake 22

North Cascades
http://www.wta.org/go-hiking/hikes/lake-22

Lake 22 is a mixture of wetlands, mountain rainforest, incredible mountain views that is easily accessible. The trail is 5.5 miles and is accessible June-October. NW forest pass required for parking.

Wallace Falls

14503 Wallace Falls Rd. Gold Bar, WA 98251
http://www.parks.wa.gov/289/Wallace-Falls

The Wallace Falls State Park Management Area is a 4,735-acre camping park with shoreline on the Wallace River, Wallace Lake, Jay Lake, Shaw Lake, and the Skykomish River. Located on the west side of the Cascade Mountains, the park features a 265-foot waterfall, old-growth coniferous forests, and fast- moving rivers and streams. Opportunities to view local wildlife, including cougar near Wallace Falls, and peregrine falcons inhabit the rock cliffs of the Index Town Wall.

The scenery is outstanding in this park, which includes numerous waterfalls, three back-country lakes, and a river. Wallace Falls drops from a height of 265-feet. The park offers a rock-climbing wall eight miles east near Index. Atop Mount Pilchuck, 60 miles away, a fire lookout provides a spectacular, panoramic view. Swimming access is five miles east at Big Eddy.

Tiger Mountain

Issaquah
http://www.wta.org/go-hiking/hikes/tiger-mountain-trail-north

Popular with weekend runners, please be respectful and keep your dog leased. This is a popular people area.

Red Top Lookout

Close to Snoqualmie pass
http://www.wta.org/go-hiking/hikes/red-top-lookout

If you are searching for a day trip with your dog, a hike to Red Top Lookout might be your perfect fit. This half-day hike rewards with stunning mountain views with minimal effort. A NW Forest Service pass is required to park at the trailhead.

Spruce Railroad Trail

3002 Mt Angeles Rd, Port Angeles, WA 98362
http://www.wta.org/go-hiking/hikes/spruce-railroad

This trail is inside the Olympic National Park, one of the only national parks that allow dogs on the trails in the state. 8 miles long this hike rewards with beautiful views of one of the deepest lakes in the state, Lake Crescent. No entry fee is required.

Barclay Lake

http://www.wta.org/go-hiking/hikes/barclay-lake

This 2.2 mile trail is a perfect easy hike that leads to Barclay lake. A NW forest pass is required at the trailhead.

HIKING WITH YOUR DOG IN STATE AND NATIONAL PARKS Q & A

Pets are allowed in most state park, but must be under physical control at all times on a leash no more then 8 feet long. Owners are responsible for cleaning up after pets. Pets are not permitted on designated beaches. Pets are not allowed inside vacation homes, yurts, cabins, or other rustic structures.

Here are a few popular places to run trails or stroll with your dog:

Gifford-Pinchot National Forest

Pets are allowed in the forest, but must be kept under control or on a leash.

Lake Roosevelt National Recreation Area

Pets on a leash no longer than 6 feet are allowed in the park except in designated picnic and developed swim beach areas.

Mt. Baker-Snoqualmie National Forest

Pets on a leash are allowed on the trails and in the campgrounds, but are not permitted in swimming areas.

Mount Rainier National Park

Pets on a leash no longer than 6 feet are allowed on roads, in parking lots and campgrounds. Pets are not allowed on trails, snow, in any buildings or amphitheaters, or in the Wilderness. However, dogs on a leash are allowed on a small portion of the Pacific Crest Trail near the park's eastern boundary.

North Cascades National Park

Within the national park, pets on a leash are only allowed on the Pacific Crest Trail, and within 50 feet of roads. Leashed pets are allowed within the Ross Lake and Lake Chelan National Recreation Areas, as well as on most surrounding US Forest Service lands.

Olympic National Park

Pets on a leash are allowed in developed areas, campgrounds, at Rialto Beach to Ellen Creek, and on the Kalaloch beaches, but are not permitted on any other beaches, trails, meadows, or in any undeveloped area of the park. Pets on a leash no longer than 6 feet are also allowed on trails in Olympic National Forest.

San Juan Island National Historical Park

Pets on a leash no longer than 6 feet are allowed on all park trails and on ocean beaches in the park, but are not permitted in park buildings.

Thanks for purchasing this Blue Moth Media Guidebook.

We have several more available or coming soon.

Review Us On Amazon:

If you found this guidebook valuable, please take the time to write a review on Amazon for us. And don't forget to tell your friends to buy a copy for themselves.
http://www.amazon.com/dp/B00TFNSMOY

Where to Find the Best Products Mentioned in this book:

If you are interested in purchasing one of the products listed in this book, please check out our "Pet Store" at:
http://astore.amazon.com/jullor-20

Wholesale Orders:

Pet store-owners, dog service businesses, veterinarians, and shelters take note! If you would like to carry this book or offer it for sale during a special event Blue Moth Media would like to offer you a 40% discount on bulk orders of 10-24 books. A 50% discount will be extended on orders of 25 books or more. Alas, we cannot ship you books to sell on consignment.

Please contact *bluemothmedia@yahoo.com* for more information.